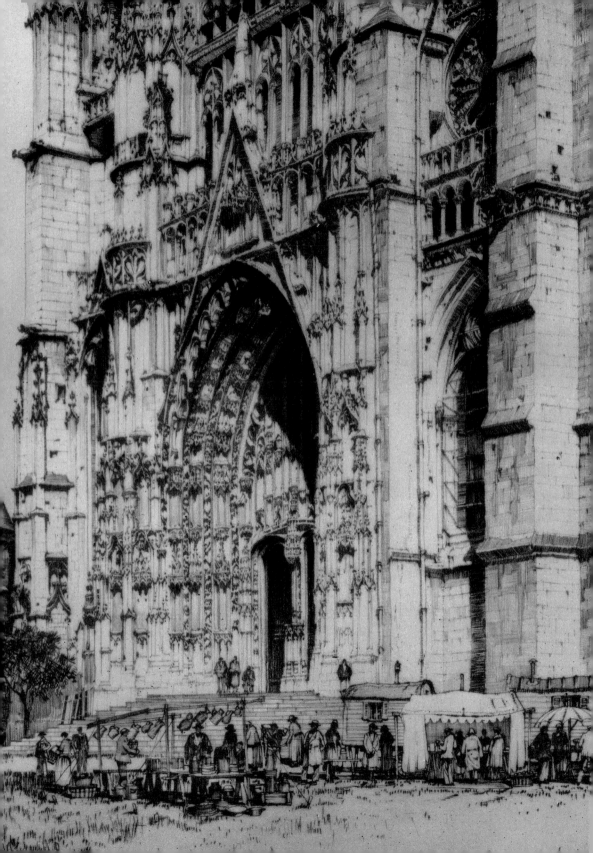

The Manoir de Raray

France
WILL LIVE AGAIN

The Portrait of a Peaceful Interlude
1919-1939

Drawn with ETCHINGS, LITHOGRAPHS,
SKETCHES *and* PHOTOGRAPHS *by*

Samuel Chamberlain

WITH AN INTRODUCTION BY

Donald Moffat

HASTINGS HOUSE   *Publishers*   NEW YORK

RUE DE LA BUCHERIE - PARIS.

First Printing, December 1940
Second Printing, December 1940

FRANCE WILL LIVE AGAIN

A Table of Contents

RUE SAINT
SEVERIN
PARIS

Introduction

You would have to look hard to find a man better equipped than Samuel Chamberlain to make a book of this kind; he might have been designed by nature and training for the job. Many men and women—including many artists—have exposed themselves to Europe over periods much longer than the fifteen-odd years he spent there, and brought back nothing comparable, in work and knowledge, to show for it. Chamberlain merely took the whole of France for his *atelier;* in it he won not only his present distinction as an etcher, but something else almost equally significant from the artist's point of view: a profound and sympathetic understanding of France and its people and their way of life.

He first went abroad in 1917, when he cut short his architectural studies to join the French Army as an ambulance driver. And in France—after a short interval at home when the war ended—he remained for good. He bought an old Ford and wore it out on the French roads; then, in a new Fiat, which gradually turned into an old Fiat as a wife and later two little girls were added to the strength, he rolled up the kilometres poking into every corner of France, etching, taking photographs, sketching and, wherever he went, absorbing France and making friends. It would be no exaggeration to say that in the process he became part French himself,—French, it may be owned, by saturation: for his reputation in the so-called minor field of food and wine is as sound as in the graphic arts.

His affection for the French and his respect for their way of living triumphantly withstood the superficial annoyances of life in that charming but occasionally vexatious land. Notably they survived the trials of owning a piece of it,—a tribute, I think, to his indomitable modesty. For when the children reached school age, he bought an old house with a walled garden in Senlis in the Oise, and with his wife made it charming. The historic saga of the Chamberlain house is an epic that some day must be related. If he never tells it, it will not be for want of documentation: the *dossier* was a foot thick and already known as the Leaning Tower of Senlis when I last saw it several years ago. Reading like a rogues' gallery of scampish *ouvriers, entrepreneurs, fonctionnaires, avocats, notaries, huissiers, architectes-vérificateurs, percepteurs,* and their bloodthirsty brethren of high and low degree, the *dossier* is a play-by-play account of an adventure into darkest *papperaserie* that would have soured forever a nature less patiently understanding or a

5

lover less devout. Yet Chamberlain not only survived the experience but emerged from the jungle of forms, appeals, summons, *jugements, impots,* bills, receipts, and declarations his serene and magnanimous self, every illusion in place. The Chamberlains have lost—probably—nothing but the house itself; but for this they feel amply recompensed by the memory of their happy years behind its stout stone walls, and by the many other varieties of coin which constitute a medium of exchange made nowhere but in France. There is no estimating the fund of gratitude they earned in those days from wandering Americans. As unofficial *concierge* of Senlis, and as the most subtly gifted host I have ever known, Sam Chamberlain provided advice and sympathy and comfort for throngs of bewildered compatriots who—like my own family—found sanctuary there from time to time under his generous wing.

Chamberlain knows France, inside out. He has observed it through a humane and civilized eye, portrayed it with an artist's hand; and here he has chosen from his portfolio a characteristic record of remembered beauty. It is a remembrance indeed, and a prophecy as well; its maker's tribute to the France of yesterday and a testament of his faith in the France that one day will rise again. We see her now through a dark and tragic veil through which few gleams of light escape,—a fabric which those of little understanding take for a burial shroud, but a garment from which France, when the time comes, will know how to fashion a pair of strong and graceful wings to soar again into the upper light where she belongs.

What is the miracle of France? What has made her blessed? Racial generalizations are risky things. Yet if one were to take the plunge, and select a single characteristic from the many that go to make up that complex individualist, the average Frenchman, one would have to choose intelligence. The clear light of reason, logic, intellect,—call it what you will,—is the flame he instinctively trusts and follows. From it is kindled the originality of his art, the integrity of his craftsmanship. Just as the artists whom France honors most highly are those who show intellectual originality (the French have little use for old models), so her craftsmen are incapable of fulfilling their primary utilitarian function without expressing themselves in designs of beauty. Beauty and integrity are one. Each, artist and craftsman, conceives his task not in terms of mystical inspiration, but as an exercise in pure reason. With his hands and with his heart, the typical Frenchman uses his head.

The story of Robert Bruce and the spider, a Scottish fable, could not, for instance, have been invented by a Frenchman. Robert's behavior was not *raisonnable.* You remember the tale: six times defeated by the British, deserted by his followers and on the point of giving up the campaign, he lay hidden in the tower of a Highland castle when his eye

6

chanced to fall upon a small spider spinning its web high in the corner between wall and ceiling. Six times the insect flung its gossamer across the gloomy firmament, and six times it failed to find an anchorage. Patiently, and without varying its method a jot, it tried a seventh time—and the filament held! The Bruce, inspired, went forth to rally his men and defeat the enemy,—using, no doubt (though the fable doesn't say so), exactly the same tactics that had six times failed.

Ever since that time and probably before, this has been the favored British method of overcoming difficulties, the method in fact which has made the Empire mighty. "If at first you don't succeed, try, try again," and "a man who doesn't know he's licked is never beaten" together spell the traditional Briton.

The Frenchman, if at first he doesn't succeed, puts his wits to work and thinks of a better way. He considers the British method neither reasonable nor intelligent. The Englishman for his part secretly thinks that a race that has to depend on brains for success, instead of on dogged perseverance, is somehow lacking in character, in that moral toughness which—believe the British—turns flabby unless taken out regularly and given exercise. Undoubtedly the collapse of France surprised the British less than it did the French. And if Great Britain in turn should fall, the French will be less astonished than the British. France has been conquered, but not destroyed. If Britain is beaten it will have been by destruction alone. One suspects that they would rather have it so.

Though for these and similar reasons the two races have never really understood one another, they do acknowledge a genuine mutual respect. The contempt which France has always entertained for Germanic civilization, and which was one of the underlying reasons for her defeat, is not felt towards England. The English, believe the French, though sometimes stupid, are nevertheless essentially civilized. Whereas Germany, for all her intelligence, is culturally and by natural inclination still barbaric. How could a Frenchman, that supreme individualist, feel anything but contempt for a race that, however skilled mechanically, actually *likes* to drill, to march, to keep step by regiments? "Ever since Germany has been an empire there has been nothing anybody wanted to buy and after having bought wanted to leave to a museum, neither music nor pottery nor poetry, and so there is something wrong," wrote Gertrude Stein. Could this be said of France at any time in her history?

A dull building in France is a rare object. However humble or glorious it may be— peasant's cottage or cathedral—traces of creative workmanship may nearly always be found in its stone or wood or ironwork. This is not the result of mere chance: the French artisan has always liked to express himself in his work, to flirt with it a little for the sake of amusement and to gratify his sense of artistic achievement.

7

You will see on the title page a battered copper *Coq Gaulois* with the word *Bétourné* thrice inscribed on it. This weather-worn bird has spent the last four hundred years— except for the three times it has been taken down for repairs—perched on the tip of Senlis cathedral's spire. On each occasion the repairs were made by a Bétourné, a family of Senlis tinsmiths; and each of the three signed his name to his work. No doubt they did it as much for fun as from pride of craft: it amused them to give the gallant old cock a personal touch.

Turn to the château of Anne de Bretagne at Gien, on page 169, and count if you can the number of different brick patterns in its façade. Examine the Renaissance Hotel de Ville at Compiègne on page 73. At first glance it appears to be a perfectly symmetrical composition in stone,—till you study it closely and discover the infinite variations in its architectural detail. There was certainly a great gulf between the architect of Compiègne and the forgotten smith who wrought the iron grille gateway of Corneuil on page 100; yet both of them succeeded in avoiding dull mechanical symmetry while achieving an appropriately balanced design. On the same page you will find a drawing of a Normandy *chaumière*, or thatched farmhouse, part brick, part stone, part timber and plaster. One half of the roof is tiled; the other is thatched, and wears a jaunty plume of weeds on its rooftree. This farmhouse is no more; it was torn down between wars. But it is likely that nobody, least of all the occupants, could say how old it was or when its transformations were effected. As it stood, it was a perfect example of the French genius for blending different materials and styles into a harmonious whole. The result was a house both pleasing to the eye and thoroughly livable,—because the men who did the work, though of different generations, had all the French craftsman's instinct for good design.

Many of the other lovely old buildings shown in these pages—their beauty mellowed and softened by the gentle finger of time—now lie in fragments, victims of the German *Blitzkrieg*. When an old house falls something goes out of the heart, something that at first seems irreplaceable. But is it irreplaceable? A Frenchman designed and built each of them, in periods perhaps centuries apart; nobody but Frenchmen will build the new.

It may be said with truth that France has never had a "bad" period architecturally, —until she became infected with the same strange disease that in the 19th century attacked the taste and artistic integrity of all the civilized world. Nor has she ever had a single outstanding "great" period—like the Athenian, for example—which emerged in a miraculous flowering that made precedent and subsequent periods suffer by comparison. The general level of French architecture has been uniformly high throughout her history; her deeply bedded genius for design has never been uprooted and allowed to die no matter what political disorders disturbed the surface of the land. The buildings pictured in this book are proof of it. Therefore, when the time comes to rebuild, one may be sure of this: though the new designs will not reproduce or even resemble the old, the buildings that rise will be French and nothing else. Ancient traditions, old principles (not old models), adapted to new materials and new needs,—this has ever been the French way. This France, the true France, cannot be destroyed as long as the will, the spirit, the instinct for beauty and respect for craftsmanship, persist; and in the French these instincts are imperishable.

I say therefore that one may look to the future with confidence. For France draws her strength and her spirit truly from the soil, *la terre,* which alone is indestructible. That which has grown in it will grow in it again. It is the sandy plains of Bordeaux and the flinty hillsides of Burgundy that give the wines of these regions their distinction,—not the vines (which come from California), nor even the distilled knowledge and wisdom that have filtered down through generations of Bordelais and Burgundian proprietors. And as her wine, so the blood of France is drawn from the soil. There is a special and holy communion between the French soil and the French soul. Neither is complete without the other. The least mystical of races, the French are still profoundly aware of the mystical nature of this synthesis; and although they incline to speak of it in terms of money and work and bread, in their hearts they know that this union is essentially a spiritual one. If the French peasant ever forgets how much land is needed to grow the wheat to grind the flour to make a loaf of bread; if, dazzled by German mechanical adroitness and skill in organizing the human soul, he should forsake the farm for the factory,—then France will be lost indeed. She has known conquest before; but always the resurrection has taken place, and always in the characteristic form that has given the lovely syllable "France" its blessed special meaning to the world. Though resurrection be a miracle, history proves it a fact.

Few of the pictures in this book, especially the country scenes, could have been made anywhere but in France; they smell and sound and breathe of France: horses' hoofs and the slow rumble of cartwheels; the sour smell of a Breton village street and the richness of fresh bread at the baker's door; the geometry of green and brown fields inclosed by old stone; the sharp tang of the farmyard midden; the haphazard silhouette of ancient tiled roofs in a country town; arched bridges, trees rustling in carefully tended groves; the sound of bells and the sound of running water in stream and fountain and the clatter of *sabots* and voices in the village street on market day. One feels the measured pace of the seasons in town and country, the tempo of a civilization that has always known how to savor the good life, of a land whose richness has been cultivated and nourished and trusted by generations of jealous lovers. The sailor fears the sea, and justly; but the peasant trusts his land, mistrusts only his ability to give it the care it needs to keep it faithful.

When Spring comes again to her countryside, France will respond as always: with a sowing of seeds and a flowering of the spirit,—and, assuredly, as so many times in her past, with the birth of a man or woman with an Idea, through which France will again be liberated.

DONALD MOFFAT

Note

FRANCE ONCE MORE has played her historic rôle of host to the armies of Europe. It is difficult to look upon the peaceful beauty portrayed in the following pages and remember that from Hitler back to Caesar and beyond, Huns, Gauls, Visigoths, Romans, Teutons, Saracens, Moors, and Englishmen have periodically ravaged her fields and forests, burned her cities, torn and muddied and trampled her vineyards, enslaved her people, swaggered in her streets, and billeted in many of the farms and manoirs that appear in this book. Not an acre of her land or a corner of her cities but has its bloody and glorious or sordid history, its monument in stone and mortar and iron and earth to commemorate the many-chaptered history of her death, and to proclaim her invincible integrity.

Once more she lies near spiritual dissolution, once more she is calling on her last reserves of courage. All her noble history bears witness that the spirit of France, like the physical France that is shown in these pages, will again experience the miracle of rebirth. France has looked death in the face many times, and lived. France will live again.

Grateful acknowledgment is expressed to Dr. William Emerson, to the Architectural Book Publishing Co., Inc., to the editors of the "American Architect," and the editor and publisher of "Pencil Points," for permission to reproduce many of the sketches in this volume.

MANOIR DU TORDUET

List of Illustrations

The medium of each illustration is indicated by one of the following symbols:
(E) Etching; (L) Lithograph; (S) Sketch; (P) Photograph.

France—Her Villages

BURGUNDY HILLSIDE (E)   PAGE 37

Late afternoon in the village of Le Roche-pot, surrounded by ripening vineyards and dominated by its gaily-roofed château, relic of the 13th century.

THE PAINTERS' VILLAGE: MORET-SUR-LOING (Ile-de-France) (P)   38

As a shrine for artists, Moret, on the River Loing, is almost as celebrated as its neighbor Barbizon. Dungeons and fortified gates recall its medieval splendor.

THE SUNKEN VILLAGE: BOZOULS (Auvergne) (P)   38

A curious hamlet, built in the canyon eaten in the sandy rock by the River Dourdou. In its grottos Roquefort cheese is stored. Its church is Romanesque, and very lovely.

THE VILLAGE OF ST. FARGEAU (Burgundy) (S)   39

A quiet shaded *place* is found behind many a French village church, affording a playground for children and a reposeful spot for contemplative *vieillards*.

THE VILLAGE CAFE—BETHISY ST. PIERRE (Ile-de-France) (S)   39

Next to the blacksmith's shop and the *épicerie*, the café is the most universal of French village institutions. This modest establishment has prototypes in thousands of small French communities.

ANCIEN HOTEL DIEU—ST. LEU D'ESSERENT (Ile-de-France) (S)   40

This fine Renaissance structure was once the village hospital. It has suffered from neg-

13

lect since being turned into a tenement, but has lost none of its architectural charm.

THE VILLAGE GATE: TRIE CHATEAU
(Ile-de-France) (s) 41

Many such gates are still preserved in the towns of France, even though their narrow arches form bottle-necks to impede the market-day traffic. In the distance stand the towers of the 15th century château in which Jean Jacques Rousseau was once the guest of the Prince de Conti.

THE VILLAGE SQUARE: BESSE-EN-
CHANDESSE (Auvergne) (s) 42

A fortified mountain town, solid and substantial, built of blackish stone piling up into steep roofs and lofty chimneys. It was in such a village that the somber Auvergnat Pierre Laval was born.

HOT NOON IN THE MIDI: GAILLAC
(Languedoc) (s) 43

Overhanging roofs and cool arcades shelter the townspeople from the fierce sun of the south. Gaillac suffered invasions by the English in the 14th and 16th centuries. A white wine worthy of Bordeaux comes from the neighboring vineyards. The farmyards abound in the fat geese that lay down their livers to the greater glory of the Christmas feast.

THE HARNESS SHOP (In a Normandy
Village) (E) 44

The versatility of the French country store-keeper is demonstrated by the advertisements on the front of this ancient half-timbered shop. Though his staple article of commerce appears to be horse collars, he is prepared also to supply groceries, drygoods, harness, saddlery, grain and feed, coffee, cider, liqueurs, wine,

and tobacco,—not to mention the jars of candy and paintbrushes displayed in the window.

NORMANDY COTTAGE (s) 44

This miniature timbered *chaumière*, secure behind its hedge, faithfully symbolizes the life of the hard-working Norman peasant.

AUBERGE DU VIEUX PUITS: PONT
AUDEMER (Normandy) (s) 45

This picturesque old building of timber, brick, and stone was formerly a tannery. To-day—as the suspended signboard points out —it is ready to provide shelter for travelers on foot or on horseback, and offers them such tempting dishes as *poulet à la Vallée d'Auge* and *escalope de veau à la Normande*. Behind the house lies a richly atmospheric courtyard, once lined with tanning sheds.

THE VERDANT VILLAGE: MIDSUM-
MER AT BELLEFONTAINE
(Ile-de-France) (E) 46

Bellefontaine in the Oise is a familiar type of country village. Half submerged beds of watercress lie in the foreground. Beyond the church tower grow the great oak trees which form the *parc* of the village château.

THE SNOW-CAPPED VILLAGE: MID-
WINTER (Comté de Nice) (P) 46

The close-built village of St. Etienne-de-Tinée, in the Alpine foothills, lies close to the Italian frontier. The popular ski resort of Auron is on a neighboring plateau.

BRETON VILLAGE: GUIMILIAU (P) 47

Whitewashed walls, and doors and windows framed in rich brown stone provide the architectural motif of the typical Breton village. The churchyard gate leads to one of the most celebrated *calvaires* in all France. This village

boise, chiefly renowned for its magnificent château, was also the scene of the massacre of the Huguenots, which took place in the presence of the court, including Francis II, Mary Queen of Scots, Catherine de' Medici, and her two sons. Leonardo da Vinci, summoned to Amboise on a commission by Francis I, died here in 1519.

France — Her Towns and Cities

LISIEUX (Normandy) (E)   57

Lisieux, the ancient Gallo-Roman town of Noviomagus, capital of Lexovii, was the home of the beloved Ste. Thérèse, "The Little Flower." Some of the most extraordinary timbered houses in France are clustered in its narrow streets, particularly in the Place Victor Hugo, where this drypoint was made.

MARKET DAY IN BOURGES

(Berri) (s)   58

Encroaching houses make it impossible to obtain a clear view of the whole façade of Bourges Cathedral. One of the finest Gothic structures in all Europe, it is built on the unique five-aisle plan, and its stained glass is excelled only by that of Chartres. The North Tower, seen at the left in this drawing, is the famous *Tour de Beurre*. Bourges, capital of the Berri, was ancient Avaricum, sacked by Julius Caesar in 52 B. C. Euric, King of the Visigoths, Clovis, Pepin-the-Short, and the Normans captured and pillaged it in turn. Though it has been the victim at various other times of religious warfare, fire, and pestilence, Bourges still nobly survives.

SILHOUETTE OF SENLIS

(Ile-de-France) (E)   59

Senlis owes its somewhat spiny silhouette to the large number of churches that overpopulate this former ecclesiastical capital. Many of them are now disaffected and serve as carpenter shops, cinema houses, and vegetable markets. French kings from Clovis to Henri IV resided in the ancient château of Senlis.

OLD ANGERS (Anjou) (s)   59

This enchanting town is distinguished by its fine timbered houses, the gray slate of its roofs, and for the soft wines of the region. The capital of Anjou—and recently too the capital of Poland in exile—suffered severely during the English invasions of the 15th century. Commercially it is headquarters for the hemp and linen industries, and is also the home of Cointreau.

THE MASON'S HOUSE: SENLIS

(Ile-de-France) (E)   60

The cloisters of what used to be the Hôtel Dieu, or town hospital, for many years served Senlis's leading stone mason as a storage place for his scaffolding, ladders, and carts. The building was recently converted into a museum for sculptural relics.

HOTEL ST-POL: ROMORANTIN

(Orléanais) (s)   61

A noble old 15th century house of stone and timber and patterned glazed brick whose bright colors have faded into an opalescent tapestry. Romorantin was familiar to thousands of American doughboys who were billeted in neighboring Gièvres during the last war.

OLD HOUSES OF DINAN

The sagging timbers of these 16th century houses have resulted in a tipsy, almost violent picturesqueness. A feudal stronghold, this ancient walled town was burned by the English in 1344, and again in 1364, when its fate was decided by the famous duel between Du Guesclin and Canterbury.

FARM GATE IN THE OISE

THE RIVERBANK: GIEN

Many of the towns in the heart of France grew up, like Gien, along the banks of a quiet river. The little three story buildings house the town's butchers and bakers and candlestick makers, the bicycle repair shops and café keepers, who carry on their trades on the ground floor and lodge their families in the apartments above. Behind this particular group rises the majestic shape of the Château d'Anne de Bretagne.

LA MAISON DU COLOMBIER:

Steep roofs, a touch of architectural fantasy, and an impression of plenty are all apparent in many of Beaune's old houses. Capital of a land of good food and excellent wines, Beaune is one of the most satisfying of French provincial towns.

THE WINE MERCHANT'S HOUSE:

LA CHARITÉ-SUR-LOIRE

Gargantuan chimneys and high-pitched roofs dwarf the delicate Gothic detail over the windows of this ancient dwelling. The buttressed wall at the left shows that the roof was once even higher than it is at present. Under the house lie capacious wine cellars.

THE ROOFS OF SELESTAT

Here are some interesting geometrical fragments of interlocking masonry.

TIMBERED VETERANS: SAUMUR

A rather "busy" subject in the heart of the inner town. Saumur is known chiefly for its majestic château, on the banks of the Loire, and for its cavalry school. The wines of the district, still or naturally sparkling, are esteemed for their clean and palatable qualities. Saumur was the home of the cynical revolutionary financier Joseph Foulon, who remarked: "If the people cannot find bread, let them eat hay." He was hanged in 1789 by a Paris mob, with an appropriate handful of hay in his mouth.

SKYSCRAPERS OF MENTON

Overlooking Menton's picturesque fishing port, this imposing pile of masonry lies near the eastern end of the town, within a short distance of Garavan and the Italian border. Menton formerly belonged to the Principality of Monaco, and was annexed by France in 1861.

Abbeville has long been a favorite of black-and-white artists as one of the most sketchable towns in France. Five contiguous cafés, silhouetted against the imposing profile of the Eglise St. Vulfran, are crowded into the central buildings. The tempestuous sky in this drawing recalls tragic events in the town's recent history. Abbeville lived under English domination, too, for nearly two hundred years. Here in 1514 Louis XII was married to Mary Tudor, sister of England's Henry VIII; and here the leaders of the first two crusades made rendezvous.

GABLES OF COLMAR (Alsace) (E)   68

An entertaining variety of roof-lines distinguishes the architecture of this historic town. Colmar was the home of Martin Schoengauer, great German painter of the 15th century.

THE SHADOWY STREET: SENLIS

(Ile-de-France) (E)   68

At the foot of the street is the disaffected church of St. Aignan, now the town cinema.

TOUR DE L'HORLOGE: RIOM

(Auvergne) (P)   69

It is in this judicial center, seat of the Cour d'Appel and of the Cour d'Assizes du Puy-de-Dôme, that trials are being held to determine the war-guilt of the French politicians and generals. The octagonal tower dates from the 16th century.

COURTYARD OF THE HOSPICE DE

BEAUNE (Burgundy) (P)   70

This famous hospital and home for the aged, still administered by the *Réligieuses*, was founded in 1443 by Nicolas Rolin, Chancellor of Burgundy. Its courtyard, built in the Flemish style, is the scene of the annual *vente aux enchères* when the wines from the numerous vineyards belonging to the Hospice are sold at auction.

CONCARNEAU (Brittany) (P)   71

An unusually picturesque overhanging house even for Concarneau, whose narrow streets and brilliantly colored fishing fleet have been for generations favorite subjects for painters. This house is on the rue Vauban in the *Ville Close,* an island stronghold entirely surrounded by massive granite walls. It dates from the 14th century, when the British were besieged here by Du Guesclin.

THE BANKS OF THE EURE: CHAR-

TRES (Orléanais) (P)   72

From the banks of this quiet stream, used as a laundry by the townspeople, the famous cathedral appears in novel and unusually beguiling perspective.

THE LOWER TOWN: CHARTRES

(Orléanais) (P)   72

The apses of St. Pierre (c. 1150-1225) and the 16th century St. Aignan dominate the background of this view made from the ancient fortifications.

THE HOTEL DE VILLE: COMPIEGNE

(Ile-de-France) (P)   73

The historic part played by Compiègne in the last two wars can hardly be forgotten. Its early 16th century town hall—light-hearted, richly ornamented, and capped by a fanciful belfry—is a unique example of Gothic civil architecture. Compiègne was a favorite country residence of the Kings of France. Here in 1430 Jeanne d'Arc was taken prisoner by the Burgundians.

THE TWO-STORIED WELL: GIEN

(Orléanais) (P)   74

An architectural rarity found in an out-of-the-way courtyard and photographed in the rain. In its oaken bucket water may be lifted to either level.

THE BANKS OF THE LOING:

NEMOURS (Ile-de-France) (P)   75

A 12th century château and a street of overhanging houses are reflected in the most peaceful of streams. One of America's great industrial families traces its ancestry back to Nemours.

France — Her Cathedrals and Churches

contrast pleasantly with the elaborate carving, reminiscent of certain examples of Spanish Gothic.

CHURCH OF THE MADELEINE:
VERNEUIL-SUR-AVRE
(Normandy) (E) 84

This magnificent tower is the focal point of all the roads leading into Verneuil from the surrounding countryside. Built between 1506 and 1536, it rises two hundred feet above the rooftops of its quiet Normandy town in a thrilling crescendo of Gothic detail. The extra buttressing on the north side gives it an asymmetrical design,—yet it bears a striking resemblance to Rouen Cathedral's *Tour de Beurre*. Henry I of England made Verneuil a fortress in 1119, and here in 1424 a bloody battle was fought between the French and English.

MARKET DAY IN LILLEBONNE
(Normandy) (E) 85

This surprising 16th century church represents the very pinnacle of asymmetrical design. Repeatedly one element is half imbedded in its neighbor to give an effect of accidental picturesqueness that only frequent alterations could have achieved. The remains of a Roman theatre built in the reign of Hadrian is a reminder that Lillebonne was once the ancient Roman town of Juliobona.

EGLISE STE. CROIX: LA-CHARITÉ-
SUR-LOIRE (Nivernais) (E) 86

One of the pleasantest towns of the Upper Loire, La Charité is rich in examples of Romanesque architecture, among which this Norman church tower is an outstanding specimen.

THE CATHEDRAL OF ST. CORENTIN:
QUIMPER (Brittany) (E) 87

The spiny Gothic cathedral and fantastic houses of the Rue Chapeau Rouge have been painted, etched, and drawn by generations of artists. A vast construction scheme undertaken in the mid-19th century and paid for by public subscription makes St. Corentin an unusually finished example of Gothic architecture.

CATHEDRAL SPIRES: ANGERS
(Anjou) (E) 88

A musty street of old timbered houses contrasts sharply with the recently restored spires of Angers' 12th-13th century Cathedral of St. Maurice.

THE SUNLIT TOWER: CHURCH OF
ST. MARTIN, COLMAR (Alsace) (E) 89

This fine and dignified French Gothic tower is topped by a bit of tasteless *chinoiserie* that betrays the heavy hand of its German designer and reminds us of Colmar's frequent changes of allegiance in the past. The church stands on the site of a Romanesque basilica of the 10th century. Destroyed by fire in 1575, it was later rebuilt of a local stone that presents a variety of warm browns, reds, blues, and slate-greens.

SENLIS FROM A CROW'S NEST
(Ile-de-France) (E) 90

The Norman Cathedral of Senlis from the tower of the Church of St. Pierre, which is now used for a covered market. The 13th century spire suffered eight direct hits in the War of 1914-1918, and was restored in 1932. The building in the foreground is the Civil Tribunal.

set in thick, austere walls, are the hallmark of its 12th century builders.

THE CHAPEL: ABBAYE DE MONT-
MAJOUR (Provence) (P)   99

This serenely isolated chapel was built by the Abbé Rambert in the 11th century to commemorate a victory over the Saracens. The four rounded apses give it a plan in the shape of a four-leaf clover.

TOUR MAGNE: NIMES (Languedoc) (P) 99

In Roman times, Nîmes was encircled by ninety towers, of which this indestructible pile of masonry is the sole survivor.

SNOW-CAPPED CHAPEL: ST. ETIENNE-
DE-TINEE (Comté de Nice) (P)   100

AN ISOLATED CHAPEL NEAR SERANON
(Provence) (P)   100

CATHEDRAL NOTRE DAME: RODEZ
(Gascogne) (P)   101

Though this powerful symphony in golden stone was begun in 1277, the façade was not completed for nearly two hundred and fifty years. The rose window, which is in the flamboyant tradition, shows traces of the Renaissance in its final cresting.

THE MAUSOLEUM: ST. REMY
(Provence) (P)   10.

On the plateau outside this dusty little Midi town stand two surprising relics from the Roman town of Glanum, still in an excellent state of preservation. Their comparative crudity seems to date them after the time of Constantine. The four magnificent bas-reliefs on the outer walls represent a cavalry skirmish, a hunt, the death of Patrocles, and the combat of the Amazons.

TRIUMPHAL ARCH: ST. REMY
(Provence) (P)   10.

Framed in cedar and olive trees, the ruin of the arch still reveal a handsomely coffered vault to recall once again Roman skill in stone cutting.

CHAPEL AT LE MOURRET, NEAR
TARASCON (Provence) (P)   10

THE TOWERS OF ROUEN
(Normandy) (P)   10

Another view of the famous *Tour de Beurre* with the cathedral's spectacular iron spire piercing the top of the picture.

France — Her Varied Shore

SAILORS HOME FROM THE SEA:
ETRETAT (Normandy) (E)   105

Picturesque notes of this pebbly strand are the *caloges,* or old fishing boats, long since retired from active duty and beached to serve as storage places for nets and gear, and as models for Etretat's summer colony of painters. In the background rise the chalk cliffs, some of them pierced by natural arches. Behind the little chapel on the hill stands a flat monument to mark the place from which Nungesser and Coli

took their departure on their ill-fated Atlantic flight. Isabey painted often in Etretat, and made many lithographs of its cliff scenes. The town was a favorite of Guy de Maupassant and Alphonse Karr.

FISHING FLEET: CONCARNEAU
(Brittany) (P)   10

The brilliant panorama of many-colored sails, spars, and rigging has made Concarneau a favorite spot for generations of painters. The slender poles are part of the tuna fisherman's gear.

When the ships come in with a fresh haul the quais of Concarneau present a lively scene. Every available Breton fisherman is pressed into service to get the catch ashore and on its way to the canning factories as quickly as possible.

The sunny peace of the beaches of Dieppe in 1938 evoke another picture: the shallow, shelving beach of Dunkirk in the spring of 1940. The sands of Normandy have seen fighting ever since Dieppe was first colonized by Norse rovers in the 10th century. Dieppe's ancient château stands at the head of the steep cliffs near the spot from which this view was made.

Commerce moves at a leisurely pace among the inlets of Brittany.

Her fleet of more than eight hundred vessels made Douarnenez, in the days before the war, the leading fishing port of France. The daily harvest of tuna, sardines, mackerel, and langouste was sent express to the Paris market.

Two Italian vessels drying canvas after a rainy night. This picture was taken in January, 1939, on the very day the two boats cleared for Italy loaded down with French scrap iron.

New-fangled methods have never gained a foothold in ancient Douarnenez. Ships are un-loaded by man power, and the fish, two in each hand, carried up the ramp by a chain of fishermen.

This fragment of Concarneau's massive granite *Ville Close* might almost be described as a fortified clock.

The quais of this Mediterranean port, founded in the early fourteenth century by Charles II of Anjou, are lined with buff, pink, and orange houses whose windows are usually decked with bright garlands of washing. The aroma of this particular quarter is pronounced and hearty. Most of Villefranche's streets consist of stone stairs.

Low tide in one of the most charming of all Brittany's little ports. Near Quimper.

Before the present war Villefranche was the home port of our Mediterranean fleet. Sections of the *Moyenne Corniche*—one of three highways that dramatically skirt the precipitous Riviera shore—can be seen against the face of the wooded cliffs in the background.

In 1939 this sea-girt fort added a fresh chapter to its history by serving as barracks for a regiment of *Chasseurs Alpins*.

WATERCOLOR SUBJECT: ANTIBES
(Comté de Nice) (P) 114

The entrance to this sheltered harbor is marked by a shining lighthouse at the end of a mole constructed by Vauban. Beyond is the old *Fort Carré*.

DRYING NETS: ANTIBES
(Comté de Nice) (P) 114

A sober and hard-working port is Antibes, in contrast to its frivolous neighbor, Juan-les-Pins.

France — Her Countryside

MIDSUMMER SILHOUETTE: NEAR SENLIS (Ile-de-France) (E) 115

THE COUNTRY ROAD: ST. FIRMIN (Ile-de-France) (E) 116

This bit of rural France lies not far from the château formerly used as a country place by Ambassador Bullitt.

VILLERS ST. PAUL (Ile-de-France) (S) 116

THE SAPLINGS (E) 117

Near Verberie, in the Oise. The lacy edge of a forest, rolling fields, and a distant spire form a composition utterly and characteristically French.

PIGEONNIER (S) 117

PIGEONNIER: BOUCHOU (Languedoc) (S) 118

The slow lichen of centuries has stained the weathered brick of this old pigeonnier hidden away on a Midi farm. The small turrets are architectural rarities in this type of building.

HAYSTACK IN THE MAKING: NEAR BEAUVAIS (Ile-de-France) (P) 118

The peace and security of this scene—so typically French in each detail—touch the heart with nostalgia.

THE CHALKY ROAD: PONT LEVOY (Touraine) (P) 119

No element of the countryside has the power to stir the imagination more vividly than one of the receding white roads of France.

FRENCH SKIES: ST. PERAVY-LA-COLOMBE (Touraine) (P) 120

The soul of France here finds its true expression: a church, clustering farmhouses, sunny fields and haystacks under a clear sky.

CHATEAU FARM: ST. GEORGES-SUR-CHER (Touraine) (P) 120

Another scene eloquent of France: a prosperous farm standing among rich acres of fresh-plowed loam.

VILLAGE IN THE ALPS (Comté de Nice) (P) 121

This old bridge spans a dry river-bed which turns into a roaring torrent in the rainy season.

THE DESERTED ABBEY: BRAY (Ile-de-France) (P) 122

Its fine Gothic windows blocked with masonry, this old chapel now serves as a hay-barn for one of the great farms of the Oise.

ROLLING FIELDS: NEAR FRAIZE (Lorraine) (P) 12

The neighboring Maginot Line failed to protect these carefully tended fields.

THE RAMPARTS OF CARCASSONNE (Languedoc) (P) 12

Most famous of fortified towns, seen from

outside its massive walls. Since its restoration by Viollet-le-Duc it has attracted millions of tourists who hearkened to the old precept bidding them *voir Carcassonne et mourir*.

Such a perspective, free from sign-boards, motors, telegraph poles, and similar modern blemishes, has a definitely poetic quality.

A few miles outside Arles this enormous abandoned Abbey looms over the ominous lowlands of the Camargue. Founded in Charlemagne's reign for the Benedictine monks, it has been deserted for decades. Its huge dungeon might still serve as an effective prison.

Roadside geometry of a Riviera hill town.
The little village is barely distinguishable against its background of tumbled hills.
Another view of one of Vauban's fortified towns and its magnificent valley. German officers were imprisoned in the lofty château-fort during the first World War.

France — Her Bridges

The glorious red-brick town of Albi silhouetted against a late afternoon sky. The Vieux Pont, in the foreground, has seven unequal arches of weathered brick and stone that still provide a narrow passage for horse-drawn vehicles. The skyline is dominated by France's greatest brick structure, the Cathedral of Ste. Cécile, begun in 1282 by Albi's bishop, Bernard de Castenet, and finished three hundred years later. Albi itself goes back to Celtic times.

One of the noblest monuments left by Rome, this immense aqueduct was built by order of Agrippa to bring water across the valley of the Gardon into Nîmes. Centuries of flowing waters have left deposits of lime almost a foot thick.

The massive scale of the bridge's masonry may be judged by the two small figures crossing the road. The stone, cut from a local quarry, has turned golden under centuries of Midi sunlight.

The stonework of this graceful bridge in a mountain town of the Basses-Alpes has had to be reinforced with iron.

Many Parisians consider this the most beautiful of the Seine's many lovely bridges. Meryon etched it with consummate artistry, and it has been painted times beyond number.

FANTASY OF ESTAING (Auvergne) (s) 132

An imaginary reconstruction of the old bridge over the Lot as it is said to have looked in the 13th century.

THE OLD BRIDGE: ESPALION

(Auvergne) (e) 133

One of the most perfectly proportioned bridges in France. The three arches, each of a different design, are made of a reddish stone that time has transmuted into a hundred shades of autumnal brown. It crosses the placid river Lot. In its original 13th century form this bridge was fortified with walls and towers.

THE BRIDGE AT SOSPEL

(Comté de Nice) (e) 133

This old bridge over the Bevera—also a painters' favorite—is crowned by a tower which now shelters a basket-maker's shop. Sospel, in Roman times the prosperous town of Hospitellum, stands almost directly on the frontier and at present may well be occupied by Italian troops. This is not the first indignity it has suffered. In 859 it was burned by the Saracens.

PONT VALENTRÉ: CAHORS

(Gascogne) (p) 134

Another of the famous bridges of France crosses the Lot in the bleak region of Cahors. Begun in 1308 and restored in the 19th century, this bridge is distinguished by its three fortified towers.

France — Her Cottages

THE VETERANS: JOSSELIN

(Brittany) (e) 135

The fantastic roof-lines of these sagging houses are not exaggerated. A few years after this drypoint was made the tipsy chimneys toppled and fell, the undulating roofs collapsed under their lichened slates, and the old houses were pulled down.

THATCHED COTTAGE: NOTRE DAME

DE BLIQUETUIT (Normandy) (s) 136

The soul of April Normandy is in this sketch: saplings in bud and a thorny hedge screen the time-blackened timbers of an ancient *chaumière,* whose stone foundations seem to have grown into the very soil.

COTTAGE IN JOSSELIN

(Brittany) (s) 136

Herringboned timbers set off by Breton

stonework here suggest the type of half-timbering found in England.

HOUSE IN ASPACH-LE-BAS

(Alsace) (s) 137

The snub-nosed roof gives this house the indelible stamp of Alsace. Situated as it is close to the Maginot Line, this pleasant dwelling may recently have suffered certain unplanned alterations.

STONE COTTAGE ON THE BANKS OF

THE LOIRE: NEAR SAUMUR

(Anjou) (s) 137

Typical of the soft sandstone cottages that cling to the narrow embankments of the river. In some cases the one-storey façade rises into three or more storeys in the rear, where the dike slopes away.

France — Her Farms

France—Her Manoirs

neither quite imposing enough to be ranked as a château, nor humble enough for a farmhouse.

THE PIGEONNIER: MANOIR D'ANGO,
   NEAR DIEPPE (Normandy) (s)   154

One of the most astonishingly complex bits of architecture in all France. The patterns are made up of stone, brick, and squares of flint fitted together in a dozen ingenious designs. Though the pigeonnier is the dominant element of the courtyard, the other buildings, with timber varying the stone and brick, are also of extraordinary interest. Built between the years 1530 and 1545 by an Italian nobleman named Jean d'Ango, this manoir recently served as a first-class country inn.

MANOIR DE LA HOUBLONNIERE
   (Normandy) (p)   155

This Gothic manoir-farm was a familiar landmark to travelers on the Cherbourg-Paris boat-train. The carving over the doorway has never been completed.

PIGEONNIER: FINHAN
   (Languedoc) (p)   156

A combination farm-gate and pigeonnier, lost in the Midi. The grotesque roof and stunted tree give this picture a curiously oriental effect.

MANOIR DU BOIS-DU-BAIS
   (Normandy) (s)   157

This deliberately picturesque gateway, built of checkered brick and buff sandstone, is capped by an almost unbelievable roof of enameled green, mustard, and eggshell-blue tiles, whose brilliant colors have been gradually dimmed by time and sage-green lichens. The half-timbered turret lends a final touch of fantasy to the composition. This manoir is located in a village near Cambremer, and appears to be virtually unknown.

GATEWAY: MANOIR DE CHAPEAU
   (Bourbonnais) (s)   158

The elements of this gate intersect in the best modern skyscraper tradition. Notice how the pressure on the arch has been lightened by a span of brickwork above it.

MANOIR DE CHAPEAU
   (Bourbonnais) (s)   159

A garden view of the same manoir. The bricks have turned brown and gray under centuries of weathering.

GATEWAY OF THE MANOIR D'ANGO:
   NEAR DIEPPE (Normandy) (s)   159

The entrance to the manoir shown on page 154, one of the most notable in France.

THE MANOIR DE CANAPVILLE:
   NEAR TROUVILLE (Normandy) (s) 160

As authentic and irresistibly inviting a manoir as can be found in all France. Jammed between a railroad line and a four-lane auto highway, it is a miracle that this 15th century specimen has survived. It remains, however, what it has always been: a farm. This is the type of manoir that served as model for so many of the country houses that sprang up in the American 'Twenties.

COACH-HOUSE: CORBEIL CERF
   (Ile-de-France) (s)   160

This charming example of Renaissance jewelry in stone stands on one of the pretentious estates of the Oise.

THE MANOIR DE VARMAISE
   (Ile-de-France) (s)   161

This superbly proportioned structure, which crowns a hilltop in the Oise, has come down in the world since the great days of its origin; it now serves as a storage place for farm implements and hay.

DOORWAY IN CAUDEBEC-EN-CAUX
(Normany) (s)   161
Richly carved panels of oak still ornament

this fine Gothic portal. Of the many charmin towns of the lower Seine, Caudebec is one o the pleasantest.

THE CHANCELLERIE: SENLIS
(Ile-de-France) (s)   16
Now a private residence.

France—Her Châteaux

THE ABANDONED CHATEAU:
FOUGERES (Touraine) (E)   163
This impressive edifice was sold for taxes by the owner, who nevertheless held onto the rest of the estate and rented the château lands out to farmers. Deliberately picturesque architecturally, the château has been restored by the State as a *monument historique* and opened to visitors.

CHATEAU DE FOUGERES
(Brittany) (P)   164
This massive feudal castle, as large as many a walled town, overlooks the inland town of Fougères in Brittany, and is not to be confused with the Fougères in Touraine shown on the preceding page. The château stands on a hillside above the Valley of the Nançon. Broad walks follow the line of its ramparts.

CHATEAU DE KERJEAN
(Brittany) (P)   164
Though Brittany is a province not especially noted for its châteaux, she possesses a few, like Kerjean, that rank with the finest in France. The gate in the twenty-foot-thick outer wall bears the arms of the first occupants, Louis le Barbier and Jeanne de Gouillon. The style of the château is mixed feudal and Renaissance.

CHATEAU DE VICTOT-PONFOL
(Normandy) (s)   165
A fascinatingly irregular design of stone and

brick surmounted by a pair of charming Renais sance windows.

CHATEAU GATE: FLEURIGNY, NEAR
SENS (Burgundy) (P)   16
Many of Burgundy's fortified gateways ar as interesting as the châteaux to which the lead. This photograph was taken on a sunn morning during harvest time.

CHATEAU DE MONTIGNY
(Normandy) (s)   16
A gate-house of unusual distinction give access to this dignified château.

CHATEAU DE ST. GERMAIN-EN-LIVE
(Normandy) (P)   16
The glazed brick of this gaily patterned littl building has faded to a delicate blue-green.

CHATEAU DE KERJEAN
(Brittany) (P)   16
The Renaissance well in the courtyard o this massive château, shown also on page 12 is an ingenious domed structure supported b three lichen-covered Corinthian columns.

CHATEAU D'ANNE DE BRETAGNE:
GIEN (Orléanais) (s)   16
Formal French brickwork has rarely, if eve exceeded this specimen in variety and com plexity. At least fifteen different patterns ca be distinguished in this courtyard. Though th château must have been outrageously garis when new, years of sun and rain have softene its colors into a symphony of harmonious tone

CHATEAU DE VILLEBON

(Orléanais) (P) 170

This 15th century brick château, moated and built round an inner court, is resplendent with ornamental turrets and galleries. Sully, Henri IV's powerful minister, died here in 1641.

CHATEAU DE LA GRANGE-LE-ROI

(Ile-de-France) (P) 170

A little-known château, emblazoned with bands of pink brick, located in the gently pastoral country where the famous Brie cheese is made.

THE COURTYARD: CHATEAU

D'HENONVILLE (Ile-de-France) (s) 171

Utilitarian aspect of a château-farm in the Oise, accented by a handsome pigeonnier.

CHATEAU DE ST. ELIX

(Languedoc) (s) 171

A Renaissance brick château, situated near Cazères in the Midi, standing in gardens designed by Le Nôtre. The rotundity of the towers —two of which have lost their steep roofs,— is emphasized by the plump trimmed evergreens.

CHATEAU D'ESPALION

(Auvergne) (s) 172

This serene Renaissance edifice, built on a rock on the banks of the Lot, was once the Hôtel de Ville. In the distance is Espalion's famous red stone bridge, shown also on page 133.

CHATEAU D'ESTAING (Auvergne) (s) 173

This fantastic Gothic specimen—whose proportions are not at all exaggerated in the drawing—approaches the boiling-point of picturesqueness. It dates from the 15th and 16th centuries and is at present a convent, occupied by the Sisters of St. Joseph.

MEDITERRANEAN WASH DAY

(Rear End Paper.)

CAUDEBEC-EN-CAUX

RUE DE L'ABBAYE
PARIS 1921

Index by Media

33

INDEX BY MEDIA

The Farm Gate

Burgundy Hillside (*Le Rochepot*)

France—Her Villages

The Sunken Village—Bozouls (*Auvergne*)

The Painters' Village—Moret-sur-Loing (*Ile-de-France*)

The Village of St. Fargeau (*Burgundy*)

The Village Café—Béthisy St. Pierre (*Ile-de-France*)

Ancien Hôtel Dieu—St. Leu d'Esserent (*Ile-de-France*)

The Village Gate—Trie Château (*Ile-de-France*)

The Village Square—Besse (*Auvergne*)

Hot Noon in the Midi—Gaillac (*Languedoc*)

The Harness Shop (*In a Normandy village*)

Normandy cottage

ON LOGE A PIED ET A CHEVAL

THE AUBERGE
DU VIEUX PUITS —
— PONT-AUDEMER

Auberge du Vieux Puits—Pont Audemer (*Normandy*)

The Verdant Village—Midsummer at Bellefontaine (*Ile-de-France*)

The Snow-capped Village—Midwinter at St. Etienne-de-Tinée (*Comté de Nice*)

Breton Village—Guimiliau

The Village Mill—La Mie au Roi (*Ile-de-France*)

The Village Gate—St. Jean-aux-Bois (*Ile-de-France*)

Village Street
Ammerschwihr (*Alsac*

The Village of Riquewihr (*Alsace*)

Haycart in the Sun—Eguisheim (*Alsace*)

Alsatian Back Yard—Riquewihr (*Alsace*)

Mountain Village—Lucéram (*Comté de Nice*)

The Fortified Village—Entrevaux (*Provence*)

Entrevaux and the Valley of the Var (*Provence*)

Biot Framed in Olive Trees (*Comté de Nice*)

Antique Shop—Biot (*Comté de Nice*)

Brick Gateway—Lescure (*Languedoc*)

The Town Gate—Amboise (*Touraine*)

Lisieux (*Normandy*)

France—Her Towns and Cities

Market Day in Bourges (*Berri*)

Silhouette of Senlis (*Ile-de-France*)

Old Angers (*Anjou*)

The Mason's House—Senlis (*Ile-de-France*)

Hôtel St. Pol—Romorantin (*Orléanais*)

Old Houses of Dinan (*Brittany*)

Farm Gate in the Oise

The Riverbank—Gien (*Orléanais*)

a Maison du Colombier—Beaune (*Burgundy*)

The Wine Merchant's House—La Charité-sur-Loire (*Nivernais*)

The Steep Roofs of Selestat (*Alsace*)

Timbered Veterans—Saumur (*Anjou*)

Skyscrapers of Menton (*Comté de Nice*)

Abbeville (*Picardie*)

Gables of Colmar (*Alsace*)

The Shadowy Street—Senlis (*Ile-de-Fr*

Tour de l'Horloge—Riom (*Auvergne*)

Courtyard of the Hospice de Beaune (*Burgundy*)

Concarneau (*Brittany*)

The Banks of the Eure—Chartres (*Orléanais*)

The Lower Town—Chartres (*Orléanais*)

The Hôtel de Ville—Compiègne (*Ile-de-France*)

The Two-storied Well—Gien (*Orléanais*)

The Banks of the Loing—Nemours (*Ile-de-France*)

Bird's-eye View of Senlis (*Ile-de-France*)

Gien (*Orléanais*)

Noontime in Noyers (*Burgundy*)

Auxerre (*Burgundy*)

The Yonne at Auxerre (*Burgundy*)

Church of St. Etienne-du-Mont—Paris

Old House on the Rue St. Etienne-du-Mont—Paris

Maison de la Tourelle—Paris

The South Transept—Beauvais Cathedral (*Ile-de-France*)

France—Her Cathedrals and Churches

Chartres Cathedral (*Orléanais*)

Dentelles Gothiques—Clamecy (*Nivernais*)

Church of the Madeleine—Verneuil-sur-Avre (*Normandy*)

Market Day in Lillebonne (*Normandy*)

Eglise Ste. Croix—La Charité-sur-Loire (*Nivernais*)

The Cathedral of St. Corentin—Quimper (*Brittany*)

Cathedral Spires—Angers (*Anjou*)

The Sunlit Tower—Church of St. Martin—Colmar (*Alsace*)

Senlis From A Crow's Nest (*Ile-de-France*)

The Cloister of the Cathedral—Angers (*Anjou*)

Place du Marché and the Cathedral—Senlis (*Ile-de-France*)

Churchyard Gate—St. Tugen (*Brittany*)

Calvaire—Guimiliau (*Brittany*)

Village Church—St. Herbot (*Brittany*)

The Shrine—Le Folgoët (*Brittany*)

The Lacework Façade—Rouen Cathedral (*Normandy*)

Lanhouarneau (*Brittany*)

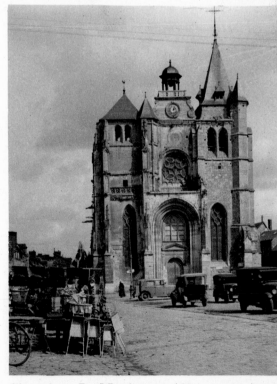

Church at Le Neubourg (*Normandy*)

Eglise Ste. Croix and the rooftops of La Charité-sur-Loire (*Nivernais*)

Leglantiers (*Ile-de-France*)

Morienval (*Ile-de-France*)

Church of St. Germain—Auxerre (*Burgundy*)

The Market Square—Nice

Abbaye du Thoronet (*Provence*)

The Chapel—Abbaye de Montmajour (*Provence*)　Tour Magne—Nîmes (*Languedoc*)

Snow-capped Chapel—Ste. Etienne-de-Tinée (*Comté de Nice*)

An Isolated Chapel near Séranon (*Provence*)

Cathedral Notre Dame—Rodez (*Gascogne*)

The Mausoleum—St. Rémy (*Provence*)

Triumphal Arch—St. Rémy (*Provence*)

Chapel at Le Mourret, near Tarascon (*Provence*)

The Towers of Rouen (*Normandy*)

Sailors Home From The Sea—Etretat (*Normandy*)

France—Her Varied Shore

Fishing Fleet—Concarneau (*Brittany*)

The Harbor—Concarneau (*Brittany*)

Low Tide—Dieppe (*Normandy*)

The Quai—Near Quimper (*Brittany*)

The Waterfront—Douarnenez (*Brittany*)

rying Sails—Villefranche-sur-Mer (*Comté de Nice*)

Tuna Fishermen—Douarnenez (*Brittany*)

The Harbor Clock—Concarneau (*Brittany*)

The Battered Boat—Villefranche-sur-Mer (*Comté de Nice*)

Fishing Port—Ste. Marine (*Brittany*)

The Harbor—Villefranche-sur-Mer (*Comté de Nice*)

Yachts Against the Sun—Nice

The Blue Mediterranean—Villefranche-sur-Mer (*Comté de Nice*)

Watercolor Subject—Antibes (*Comté de Nice*)

Drying Nets—Antibes (*Comté de Nice*)

Midsummer Silhouette—Near Senlis (*Ile-de-France*)

France—Her Countryside

The Country Road—St. Firmin (*Ile-de-France*)

Villers St. Paul (*Ile-de-France*)

The Saplings (*Ile-de-France*)

Pigeonnier

Pigeonnier—Bouchou (*Languedoc*)

Haystack in the Making—Near Beauvais (*Ile-de-France*)

The Chalky Road—Pont Levoy (*Touraine*)

French Skies—St. Péravy-la-Colombe (*Touraine*)

Château Farm—St. Georges-sur-Cher (*Touraine*)

illage in the Alps (*Comté de Nice*)

The Deserted Abbey–Bray (*Ile-de-France*)

Rolling Fields—Near Fraize (*Lorraine*)

The Ramparts of Carcassonne (*Languedoc*)

Route Nationale—Near Vendôme (*Orléanais*)

Abbaye de Montmajour (*Provence*)

Village Château

The Wooded Valley—Near Espalion (*Auvergne*)

Hills of Auvergne—Near Espalion (*Auvergne*)

Poplars and Shadows—Eze (*Comté de Nice*)

Foothills of the Alps—Lucéram (*Comté de Nice*)

Valley of the Var—Entrevaux (*Provence*)

Olive Grove—Near Nice

Albi Sunset (*Languedoc*)

France—Her Bridges

Pont du Gard–Remoulins (*Languedoc*)

The Stonework of the Romans—Pont du Gard—Remoulins (*Languedoc*)

The Bridge—Castellane (*Provence*)

Pont Marie—Paris

Fantasy of Estaing (*Auvergne*)

The Old Bridge—Espalion (*Auvergne*)

The Bridge at Sospel (*Comté de Nice*)

Pont Valentré–Cahors (*Gascogne*)

The Veterans—Josselin (*Brittany*)

France—Her Cottages

Thatched Cottage—Notre Dame de Bliquetuit (*Normandy*)

Cottage in Josselin (*Brittany*)

House in Aspach-le-Bas (*Alsace*)

Stone Cottage on the Banks of the Loire—Near Saumur (*Anjou*)

Cottage Gate—Corneuil (*Normandy*)

La Chaumière—Near Elbeuf (*Normandy*)

Stone and Brick Cottage—Near Vernon (*Normandy*)

Eighteenth Century House in Menilles (*Normandy*)

Near Nonancourt (*Normandy*)

The Abbey Farm—Breuil-le-Vert (*Ile-de-France*)

France—Her Farms

Romanesque Farmyard—Cousnicourt (*Ile-de-France*)

Farmyard near St. Witz (*Ile-de-France*)

Farm Vista—Le Plessis-Luzarches (*Ile-de-France*)

Farmyard—St. Leu d'Esserent (*Ile-de-France*)

Homecoming—Cressonsacq (*Ile-de-France*)

The Farm's Formal Façade—Near Provins (*Ile-de-France*)

Brick Farmhouse Framed in Stone—St. Rémy-en-l'Eau (*Ile-de-France*)

Hillside Farm near Espalion (*Auvergne*)

Stone Farm near Tréogat (*Brittany*)

Farm Gate—St. Jean-aux-Bois (*Ile-de-France*)

Pigeonnier—Cousnicourt (*Ile-de-France*)   Gateway at Balagny (*Ile-de-France*)

The Chateau Farm—Le Plessis-aux-Bois (*Ile-de-France*)

Voisinlieu (*Ile-de-France*)

Montepilloy (*Ile-de-France*)

Barn at Douains (*Normandy*)

Hilltop Farm—Angély (*Burgundy*)

Courtyard in St. Raphael (*Provence*)

Feudal Farm—Asquins, near Vézelay (*Burgundy*)

Normandy Farm—Les Loges, near Lisieux

The Manoir at Préaux (*Normandy*)

France—Her Manoirs

Manoir de Raray (*Ile-de-France*)

The Pigeonnier—Manoir d'Ango, near Dieppe (*Normandy*)

Manoir de la Houblonnière (*Normandy*)

Pigeonnier—Finhan (*Languedoc*)

Manoir de Bais (*Normandy*)

Gateway—Manoir de Chapeau (*Bourbonnais*)

Manoir de Chapeau (*Bourbonnais*)

Gateway of the Manoir d'Ango—Near Dieppe (*Normandy*)

The Manoir de Canapville—Near Trouville (*Normandy*)

Coach House—Corbeil Cerf (*Ile-de-France*)

The Manoir de Varmaise (*Ile-de-France*)

Doorway in Caudebec-en-Caux
(*Normandy*)

The Chancellerie—Senlis (*Ile-de-France*)

The Abandoned Château—Fougères (*Touraine*)

France—Her Châteaux

Château de Fougères (*Brittany*)

Château de Kerjean
(*Brittany*)

Château de Victot—Ponfal (*Normandy*)

Château Gate—Fleurigny, Near Sens (*Burgundy*)

Château de Montigny (*Normandy*)

Château de St. Germain-en-Livet (*Normandy*)

Château de Kerjean (*Brittany*)

Château d'Anne de Bretagne—Gien (*Orléanais*)

Château de Villebon (*Orléanais*)

Château de la Grange-le-Roi (*Ile-de-France*)

I

The Courtyard—Château d'Hénonville (*Ile-de-France*)

Château de St. Elix (*Languedoc*)

Château d'Espalion (*Auvergne*)

Château d'Estaing (*Auvergne*)